art **and**
design

sculpture
&
ceramics

Chris
Dunn

Hodder & Stoughton
A MEMBER OF THE HODDER HEADLINE GROUP

Introduction

Any idea that 3D (three-dimensional) work can be appreciated simply by looking at it is far too simple. To understand 3D work we need to engage a far wider range of experiences. Large pieces demand different viewpoints, changes of perspective; they need to be walked around or revolved before you. Smaller objects are to be handled or, if functional, used. Some ceramics seem to be irresistible and cannot be properly enjoyed unless you hold them. Surface decoration can be traced over with your fingers or brushed over with your palm. Jewellery should be worn. Often the sense of touch is important, an experience described as 'tactile' and not available from all art forms. Because of this, reproductions or photographs do little to help you grasp the essential qualities of 3D work. You must plan to go out, see for yourself and, when possible, collect real objects.

George Segal (b.1924) Bus Riders, 1962, *cast from life, plaster, cottongauze, steel, wood and vinyl, 177 × 108 × 230cm, Hirshorn Museum and Sculpture Garden, Smithsonian Institution, Washington D.C.*

Form and function do not always fit together as well. Find some examples of forms which are not appropriate to their function. Examples such as shaped tea pots, face-shaped (Toby) jugs or other novelty pottery can be readily obtained. Can you think of ways that you can improve their function without losing the effect of their form? Design and produce, in any medium, a functional novelty item.

Of all the syllabus areas covered by GCSE Art and Design, the area of 3D Art and Design is the broadest. Jewellery, Sculpture, Ceramics, Stage and Theatre Design, and Product Design can all be offered in this area. With such a breadth of applications it is useful to identify the concerns that they have in common. It will help you, as technical processes become available, to consider working in a variety of applications.

When considering 3D objects the relationship between form and function needs careful consideration. Often compromises have to be made. The designer's success is in the way these two crucial elements have been balanced. Challenging design solutions are often found along the difficult dividing line between the two.

George Segal's plaster cast sculpture concentrates on form. It is a direct cast from life. Its function, though difficult to define in practical terms, is as a direct appeal to our emotions. Through it we share the artist's experiences. Dorothy Hafner has produced a bowl that fulfils its function, though its form is clearly of considerable importance. The place of decoration, especially in relation to a piece like this, is vital. Do you think this bowl would be as interesting without the bright, strident decoration applied to it?

Dorothy Hafner, Lightning Punch Bowl, with spoon, 1984, *slab formed pottery bowl.*

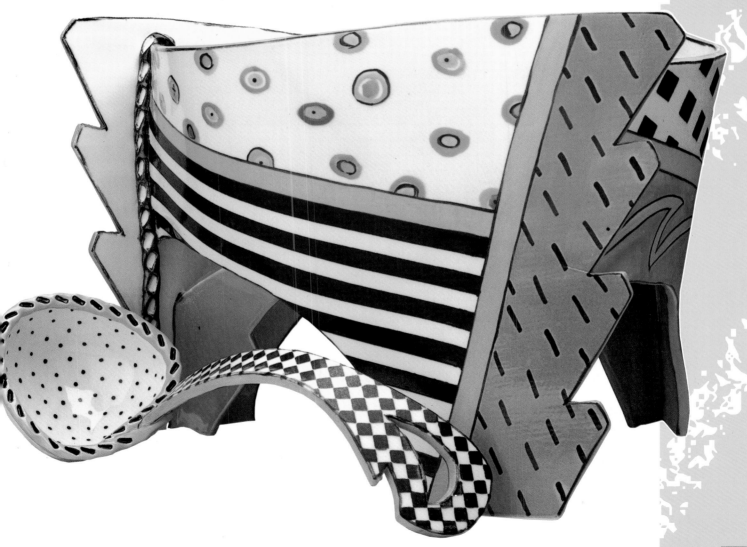

Looking at Sculpture and Ceramics

Does a work of art have to have a function? Since such works are often made for the public, should the personal satisfaction of the artist be enough? These are some of the issues that need to be debated before you go on.

Sculpture can fulfil a narrative function. It can represent a story or, as in this set of doors, tell a story rather as a cartoon or comic strip might. There is a great tradition of this type of sculpture throughout all the great cultures of the world.

The scultpures on these two pages represent two traditions of sculpture. The doors, for example, are carved; a process of removing material. The figure opposite, though cast in bronze, is based on the technique of modelling, that is adding material. These two traditional methods have been added to in recent times by the sculptor as a constructor. In this guise the sculptor creates using preformed, often industrial, materials.

Auguste Rodin (1840–1917), whose sculpture appears opposite, was the first sculptor of modern times to give sculpture the freedom often associated with painting. He enabled sculptors to make their work a vehicle for personal expression. It is as heirs to Rodin that modern sculptors are able to work. Here are some functions that a work of art might have:

To decorate.

To inform.

To commemorate a person or event.

To look good.

To make feelings or emotions come alive.

Can you think of others? Which of these functions might affect the form of the work?

Find out about other sets of doors and the stories that they tell. You could start your search looking at the doors of Florence Cathedral. Look also at the carved exteriors of Hindu temples or the layers of saints on the fronts of our Western European cathedrals.

Arowgun of Osi, Yoruba Palace **Doors,** *carved wood, 283.8 cm wide, British Museum, London.*

In 1892 Rodin was commissioned to produce a sculpture of the French writer Honoré de Balzac who lived between 1799 and 1850. Balzac produced a great series of books known as the *Human Comedy*. Rodin found the commission very difficult. All his previous work had been based on the living model. He made every effort to find out all he could about the great man. Eventually he modelled seven large nude figures and placed them around his studio. He dressed one of the figures in clothes soaked in wet plaster. The result was a figure of great strength and powerful presence. One of the masterpieces of modern sculpture, its form is as close to the 'truth' as Rodin could make it. It is a powerful representation of a great man.

But the sculpture was insulted and ridiculed. Crowds attacked it and it was considered an act of treason to show the hero, Balzac, in such an unheroic form. Rodin withdrew the piece from public view. Its function, to glorify the great man, was unfulfilled by the restrictions of public taste. It serves as an example of the violent battlelines that can be drawn between form and function.

Auguste Rodin (1840–1917),
Monument to Balzac, 1898, *cast bronze, Musée Rodin, Paris. (Detail from a photograph by Bruno Jarret).*

Find examples of public sculpture. These are often sculptures made to commemorate a life or an event. The war memorials erected after the First World War are probably the most numerous modern examples, even small villages usually have one. Make a drawn record of those you find.

Drawing for Sculpture

*Henry Moore (1898–1987),
Pencil landscape interpretation
of a drawing by Albrecht Durer,
'Portrait of Conrad Verkall',
1508, Henry Moore Foundation.*

*Take a simple, everyday
object, perhaps a kitchen
implement, and draw it from
many different angles. From
your drawings you might
isolate some part of particular
interest and, in a malleable
material such as 'cold' clay or
'new' clay, construct a small
piece of sculpture.*

Drawing is necessary as a basic preparation for sculpture, though the preparatory drawings can be quite different from those used by a painter. Often they are drawings of simple structures or individual studies, explorations to examine the possibilities of any object's form. Sometimes they are sheets which show the same element from many different angles, a sort of walk around the object.

As the scope of a sculptor's technical opportunities increases, often complex problems need to be solved. Constructional drawings, or perhaps electrical diagrams, are often necessary. Kinetic sculpture, which is sculpture that moves, or sculpture that needs special lighting, require a great deal of drawn preparation. Large works or commissions to be set on buildings may need architectural drawings that have to be very detailed.

Henry Moore (1898–1987) Intaglio Plate XXVII from Elephant Skull Album, 1970, 34.7 × 35 cm, Tate Gallery, London.

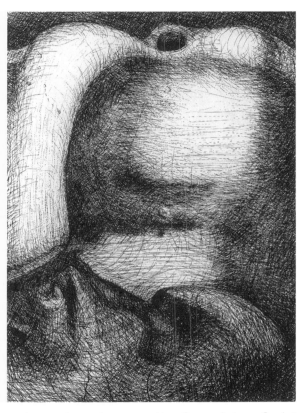

Choose a natural object, like a shell, flower head, shaped pebble or piece of bone, that can be drawn from different viewpoints. Make a series of studies, until you really feel you understand your subject. These studies might form the raw material for constructing a maquette. This might be made in card, wood or a more malleable material. You might like to experiment with combining different views that you have studied in one form. You could imagine the finished piece either as free-standing or attached to a wall.

Drawing alone is not the only preparation for sculpture. Sculptors often build maquettes. These are small scale models that can show how the finished version will look. They can be used to sort out the technical problems of structure and balance. They can show what the sculpture will look like from different angles. In public commissions they can be used to show to the patron before the work is completed, indeed this was their original function.

Some artists have built up a considerable skill in drawing as a support for their 3D work. Henry Moore, through a series of sketchbooks, developed a style of drawing well suited to the investigation of 3D form. This can be seen in the lithograph of the elephant's skull above, one of a series based on drawings. His search for form can also be seen in the other drawing opposite. From Durer's drawing he has created a landscape based on the portrait. Other examples show his versatility in drawing, a skill that has developed a considerable body of work in parallel to his sculpture.

Drawing: form

Henry Moore (1898–1987),
Shelter scene – two swathed
figures, 1941, *chalk, pen and
ink, gouache, wax crayon,
27.7 × 36.2 cm, Henry Moore
Foundation.*

One of the most critical elements in any Art & Design vocabulary is the idea of form. This element is important because it has to be controlled when working in 3D. The illusion of form also has to be created on flat surfaces. These three pieces of work in different media show how a concern for form can be represented on a flat surface.

The drawing opposite by Henry Moore shows his ability to create the illusion of form in his drawing. This ability is important for the sculptor since it has enabled Moore to visualize his work before beginning to sculpt in three-dimensional (3D) materials. In this way he could try out many more ideas quickly and accurately. Many of his important pieces can be traced back to pages of sketches like these.

He uses a wide variety of techniques in his drawings, mixing them to create this illusion of depth. Quite frequently he colours the backgrounds of his pages to allow the white of the highlights on the forms to stand out even more. The drawing above is from one of his *Shelter Sketchbooks*.

It was not meant to become a piece of 3D work, it stands on its own as a drawing of considerable value. It does however reveal Moore as an artist who has, no matter what the subject or the purpose to which his work is to be put, an overriding concern for form.

You might like to experiment with a length of white cloth and the effect it can have when used to drape a figure or group of figures. Record your experiments in a suitable way and try to make your record emphasise the form beneath the drape. If you are drawing, this could be by careful shading. Try to find other techniques for yourself by experimenting. If you choose to create your record through photography you will need to make careful use of lighting. By using cloth over the human figure you may well develop a skill in accentuating, hiding or changing the form of the figure.

The painter Rene Magritte is well known as a surrealist painter. This painting (right) has capitalised on the mystery surrounding the two wrapped figures. In doing this he has hidden the actual features but created a new interest in the form of the two. The heads are human but, in some way, mysteriously unreal.

Rene Magritte (1898–1967), The Lovers, 1928, *Richard S. Zeisler Collection, New York.*

Henry Moore (1898–1987), studies for sculpture in various materials, 1939, pencil, chalk, pen and watercolours, 25.4 × 43.2 cm, Henry Moore Foundation.

The Work Process

Grinling Gibbons (1648–1721), lime wood wreath, St. Paul's Church, Covent Garden, London.

The choirstalls of old churches or the character heads on old pipes or pottery can provide a useful starting point for head studies in wood. These can be quite small and, if properly planned, blocked out with a saw.
They could form a group portrait when mounted together. Start by drawing a series of studies to provide you with the raw material for your carving.

CARVING – A SUBTRACTIVE PROCESS

Carving is a subtractive process; material is removed until the required form is revealed. As the carving progresses so the scope for change decreases. Major changes are ruled out as the subject is blocked out (roughly carved). Detail can be developed as the form progresses. So this means that carved sculpture has to be carefully planned. Thorough preparatory drawings and sometimes maquettes are essential before carving begins.

Some common materials that can be carved are wood, stone or even concrete builder's blocks. Often the form of the original block of material plays an important part in determining the form of the final sculpture. This can be seen in the stone sculpture of some Bronze Age civilizations whose soft carving tools often leave the original block's shape. Of the materials available to students, wood is perhaps the most responsive, and the most available.

As the material is so much softer than the sharp steel carving tools, these will cut the wood with little effort. This is especially true if the tools are sharp. It is more dangerous to try and carve with blunt tools as the extra effort required to make them cut often leads to less control over where they cut! Carve where you can with the grain, use the growth of the tree to your advantage. A well planned piece of sculpture can be blocked out with a saw before you start to carve.

Though a highly finished surface is possible, as in Renonciat's work, it can be worthwhile looking at the variety of surfaces that carving can produce. A highly polished surface can bring out the colour and grain of the wood. It is possible to form a carving block by fitting together different types of wood. The different wood qualities then appear in different parts of the sculpture. You can create surface textures by leaving the characteristic marks of different chisel profiles on the surface of a finished piece.

The carving by Grinling Gibbons opposite shows his skill as a carver beyond the restrictions of the material. The wreath was carved as his memorial and so he used all his skills on it. It is so delicately carved that it seems impossible that it is carved from wood.

Christian Renonciat, bouclette, 1980, *Lebanon cedar, natural size.*

S CULPTURE & CERAMICS

Henri Gaudier-Brzeska (1891–1915), Red Stone Dancer, *1913, Tate Gallery, London.*

Choose a naturally occurring form; bird bones are a good example. Try to reproduce the forms you have found. In this way, through experience, you will quickly find the limits of your chosen material. Make a collection of your experiments, successes and failures, and choose the best. Find a way to present this piece and perhaps repeat it on a larger scale.

Find reproductions of, or visit museums where you can see, African Tribal Art. In the last half of the 19th century central Africa was being discovered by Europeans. They were interested in the exploitation of the land and its resources for their own use. They also discovered a vibrant tribal culture with strong artistic traditions of its own. Can you find examples of the effect this art had on European art? Do you think Gaudier-Brzeska might have been influenced in this way? Can you find examples of forms of sculpture that were not in use in Europe? Wooden kasks, standards and stool figures are examples, can you find others?

The doors on page 4 show that the influences of European life were absorbed by the vigorous culture of West Africa. Choose an area of Africa to investigate and see what you can find out about the art of the area.

Before you tackle stone carving, the limitations of time, cost and safety must be borne in mind. It is unlikely that you will have the time or money (yet!) to tackle a block of Italian Carrara marble so your first efforts must be more modest. Plan for a smaller work with some softer stone material. Some stones that might be available are alabaster, Bath or Portland stone, or soapstone. All these will give you the chance to obtain exciting results.

Grey cement or concrete blocks are probably the most easily obtained carving materials. These have some severe limitations but they can give you a taste of carving, and perhaps a taste for it. On a small scale detail is difficult to produce. For a beginner, however, these are ideal materials since this limitation causes a concentration on form, the essence of good sculpture. The surface of the material can be burnished to a smooth finish and can be sealed with P.V.A. or coloured with acrylic paints. Grinding powder paints into the surface as the piece is burnished will create a subtle finish. This material is invaluable as a source of experience and cheap enough to make mistakes with before you go on to something more permanent and, of course, more expensive.

Plaster, cast into a block, can also be carved. The surface can be dampened and carving with rasps and 'surform' type tools is possible. Detail can be carved in with a sharp knife or chisel, and the finished surface waxed, coated with varnish or with linseed oil. One advantage of plaster as a carving material is that it can be repaired. Quite frequently plaster is used as a maquette for investigating larger or more complex pieces of work.

Direct carving of whatever material always gives rise to dust, therefore always protect your eyes and your mouth. Goggles with safety glass are essential, and a face mask should also be worn. Try to work outside as much as possible so that these problems are limited. If you are not sure of how to go about things ask your suppliers, they are usually prepared to give advice. Noise can also be a problem both for yourself and for others. With plaster, you should avoid contact with the wet material as, when drying out, it can damage your skin. Wash your hands after you mix or pour plaster – before it dries.

Kathe Kollwitz (1867–1945), Mourning, 1938, plaster carving, Kunsthalle, Hamburg.

MODELLING – AN ADDITIVE PROCESS

Modelling is essentially an additive activity. Material is added to a basic form or support and then shaped while still soft and malleable. Clay is probably the medium most frequently modelled. Other materials used are wax, Plasticine (don't underrate it!) and some clay–type products like DAS, 'new' clay or 'cold' clay. 'Cold' clay needs to be fired when dry or it will become brittle. The 'new' clay products keep their strength when dry but they quite often shrink. They are most useful when you do not have the facility to fire clay. 'Cold' clay can be burnished to a fine, warm gloss even without a glaze. 'New' clay products have to be painted as their surface colours are often dull and uninteresting. Plasticine usually comes ready coloured.

Frequently an armature, or wire frame, is used to take the weight of a modelled piece while it is worked on, as damp material is unable to support itself. As the material dries out it becomes harder and the armature is no longer required. Armatures can often take the form of exterior supports, propping up parts of a sculpture while the material hardens. All should be removed before a 'cold' clay piece is fired or a 'new' clay piece shrinks. Quite often a work to be modelled in clay is based on a basic clay form, perhaps made from coils or slabs.

Medardo Rosso (1858–1928), Sick Man, *wax figure, The Hakone Open Air Museum, Japan.*

Henry Moore (1898–1987), a page from his "sheep" sketchbook, mainly in biro pen, Henry Moore Foundation.

Wax is a useful modelling medium which will hold fine detail. As it will not harden properly it is a relatively fragile material. Passing a candle flame over the surface will harden it to a degree, but there are obvious risks in doing that. Wax has been used by sculptors when a finer, more detailed finish was required than the body of their sculpture could provide. Hot wax was poured over the formed sculpture and the detail modelled in that. The main use for wax has traditionally been to make casts, though the artist Medardo Rosso (1858–1928) produced some startling wax figure work, as in the piece below.

Carving and modelling give contrasting results and you might like to make a direct comparison between the two ways of working. If you tackle a similar subject using the two contrasting methods you should achieve this. Produce some simple animal sculptures. Collect information, drawings or reproductions to help you. You might like to use photographs you have taken to give you the support you need. Look at sketchbooks like the 'sheep' book by Henry Moore. Look at sculpture from other periods and cultures, like Eskimo soapstone carvings, Japanese 'netsuke' or Egyptian animal gods, for inspiration.

CONSTRUCTION

As sculptors searched for new ways of expressing their needs, so new materials became available to them. Sheet steel had been cut and welded, bricks laid and electric lights lit long before they became an acceptable part of the sculptor's vocabulary. It was the sculptor's need to explore new ways of expression, in tune with the technology of our age, that led to their use in new and exciting ways. Many of these 'new' techniques were drawn from the construction or manufacturing industries. The skills used creatively by these artists were those of the factory floor. The skills employed by artists like the American, David Smith (1906–1965), were learnt in the car industry and in building railway engines. His sculptures broke new ground but his method was that of the industrial workplace. He chose and assembled parts that had been made previously.

Just as in construction or engineering projects, drawings are of crucial importance. They are essential to the planning stage. Welded sculpture has to be pre-fabricated. The sheets of metal are laid out and cut to size, often using wooden patterns. These are the techniques of the shipyard. Constructed sculpture can require technical drawings and other preparations on the same scale as might be required by an architect working on a building.

Wendy Taylor, Brick Knot, *bricks, life size, Visual Arts Library.*

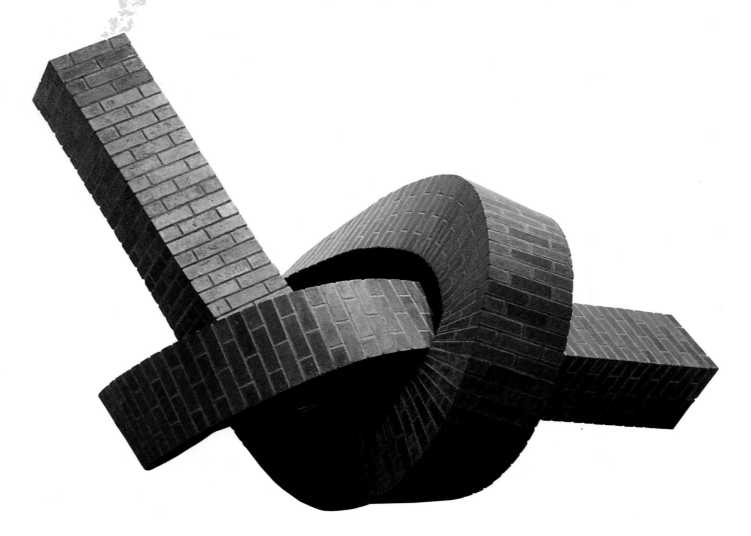

Artists like David Smith worked hard to deny the limitations of their medium. His solid welded steel forms seem to fly. A typical example is Cubi XIX in the Tate Gallery in London.

No bricklayer would create a form like Wendy Taylor's *Brick Knot* (opposite) but it shows the extent to which the medium can be stretched. Part of its impact as a piece of sculpture is the contrast between the material and the idea. The knot, usually associated with rope or some other pliable material is here recreated in a solid form. The bricks - hard, angular and pre-shaped - are formed by the artist into a dramatic curve that contradicts the qualities we know brick possesses.

Roy Lichtenstein (b.1923), in his work below, creates a similar effect. He uses a whole series of manufactured materials including hardboard and perforated zinc to freeze a moment of violent action. The solid materials and comic book colours contrast with his subject and focus our attention on it.

Construction techniques rely on the joining together of different materials. Collect together as many different materials as possible. You could join together as a group to collect and share what you glean. Construct a piece of sculpture to stand in water. Its reflection will have to be considered.

Roy Lichtenstein (b.1923), Explosion No. 1, 1965, 251 × 160 cm, Museum Ludwig, Cologne.

Form

WRAPPED FORM

*Henry Moore (1898–1987),
Crowd looking at a tied up
object, 1942, watercolour over
chalk, 40 × 55 cm, Henry Moore
Foundation.*

*Wrap up an object with a well
defined and well known form.
At what point does the item in
the package cease to be easily
identified by feeling the
parcel? You could test this
with a 'pass the parcel' type
game with your companions.
At what point do they guess
the contents of the parcel?
Draw the wrapped form.
Cloth soaked with plaster can
be used to conceal form. You
might like to use this as the
starting point for a piece of
work. Try to hide the object
from some viewpoints and yet
reveal it from others. This
way you may preserve the air
of mystery that the wrapped
form possesses.*

It should not be thought that form always has to be obvious. The wrapped form always fascinates and intrigues. Think how much more exciting it is to receive a present that has been wrapped. The practice of 'wrapping' or draping a piece of sculpture so that it can be ceremonially unveiled is a recognition of this. The painting on page 9 by Rene Magritte exploits the mystery of the veiled figure. Henry Moore returned again and again to the wrapped image in drawings like the one above. Christo and Jeanne-Claude, whose work appears on these pages, recognised the effect of this mystery. Their wrapped forms were often on an architectural scale. They therefore prepared their large works very carefully. They used maps, drawings and even photomontages, as opposite, to prepare systematically for their work. Perhaps you could use their photomontage method to examine the placing of large objects in the landscape. Find out what you can about their two very large pieces *Valley Curtain*, 1970–72, and *Wrapped Coast*, 1969. Since they are so large they could only survive as photographs or drawings. Perhaps you could produce a photomontage of a similar work on a landscape near to your home. You might like to make a landscape picture and place in it a photograph of an object obviously out of scale.

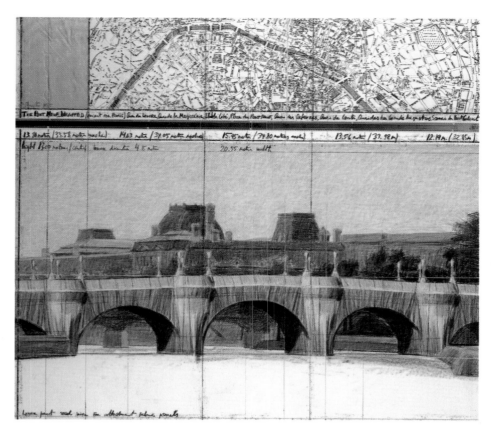

Christo and Jeanne-Claude, The Pont Neuf wrapped, Project for Paris, Drawing 1985, *in two parts: 38 × 165 cm and 106.6 × 165 cm, pencil, charcoal, pastel, crayon, map and fabric sample. (Photograph by Wolfgang Volz.)*

Christo and Jeanne-Claude, The Pont Neuf wrapped, Paris, 1975–85, *440,000 sq. ft. of woven polyamide fabric and 42,900 ft of rope. (Photograph by Wolfgang Volz.)*

ORGANIC FORM

We have looked at the way that 3D materials can be formed, how they can be changed by the additive, subtractive and constructive processes. It's worth now considering some different types of form.

Organic forms reflect those usually found in nature. They are characterised by a lack of hard edges and simplicity. The pot below, with its wide, frilled brim, seems to echo the rippling movement of a jelly fish or some other deep sea creature. The phone opposite is purely a 'fun' object. Its strange form, of which this is only a sample, adds nothing to the function of the object. The form does not suggest the object's use, in fact it is as far from the expected function of the object as it is possible to get. In this contradiction lies the phone's success.

Ursula Morely-Price (b. 1936),
Ruffle Bowl Form, 1985,
35.5 cm diameter.

Choose a simple functional object and design a 'form' for it. Make your form as unusual as you like as long as the object remains functional. You could prepare for this work by making a list of all the functional requirements of your object. This analysis could be the basis of a design brief.

Mickey Mouse telephone, British Telecom.

The sculpture above was produced as a direct challenge to the constructed sculpture of artists like Anthony Caro and David Smith. Hard-edged, flat forms that filled space but had little substance provoked a reaction in some artists who sought the opposite. Think of uses for objects that are a direct contrast to their form. As you can see from the phone, the more unlikely the use you find for your forms the more successful you could be. Support this work by drawings from life, then design functional aspects of your work.

Anish Kapoor (b.1954), Three, 1982, *wood, cement, earth and pigment, Lisson Gallery.*

OPEN FORMS

Maggie Barnes, press moulded, laminated bowl, unglazed, 1985.

Yvette Hoch, Unglazed stoneware bowl, 1985, *32 × 29 cm.*

Clay is the most malleable material. It is easily formed by hand. This means it will retain most shapes you form from it. Some forms may require support while they are damp, or even some kind of disposable support while being fired in a kiln. Usually damp clay responds kindly in the artist's hands. It is often described as a sympathetic medium; it seems to co-operate with its builder.

The bowl by Maggie Barnes has been made by pressing damp clay into a ready-made mould. The mould was made of plaster. Yvette Hoch's bowl has been made from a thick slab of clay. It has been folded up to make the bowl form.

You might like to roll out a rectangular slab of clay and allow it to dry out until it is just stiff. Fold the slab to create an open container. You could experiment to see what volume the slab can be folded to contain.

Sally Bowen Prange, edge-scape vessel, 1986, *porcelain bowl, 23 × 32 × 33 cm.*

Two basic ceramic forms are employed within the context of pottery. The open form (bowl, plate or dish) and the closed form (bottle, flask). Like many distinctions it is not fixed. Often the most interesting forms occur along the frontiers of this division.

Clay can be formed in a number of ways. These fall into two main areas. Clay can be 'thrown' on a wheel. This method uses the skill of the artist to draw the clay upwards as the potter's wheel turns. The wheel gives the power and force to the clay. The artist directs it into a form. Clay forms can also be built up by hand. Hand building includes pinched pots, slab building or forms built by coiling clay. Clay can also be pressed into pre-formed moulds.

Press a sheet of clay into a dish mould. This will give your container volume. Shape the edges of your dish by tearing, pinching, perforating, building or any other method to escape the restricted finished form of the mould.

SCULPTURE & CERAMICS

Angela Verdon, pierced bone china, symmetrical bowl, hand burnished, *11 × 7 cm.* *(Photograph by John Coles).*

Dorothy Feibleman, asymmetrical, laminated porcelain bowl, *length 10 cm.*

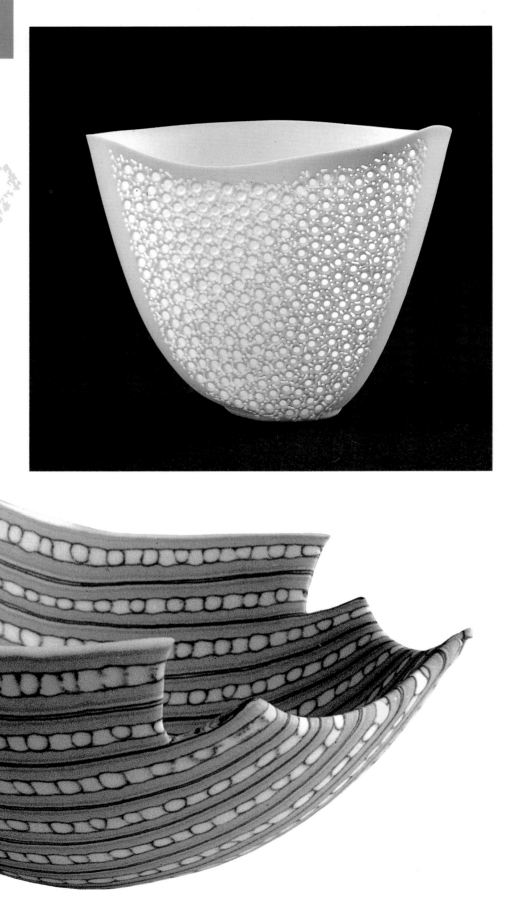

The open form is one of the most frequent functional forms. We make use of this form in everyday life. Most of the containers we use take this form; cups, saucers, plates, bowls, etc. Cup your hands together to hold water and you will see the human species' most basic container. The bowl and cup are a direct extension of this. It is no accident that the oldest pottery discovered is in this form. It may explain the pleasure that we get from a container that seems made to fit into our curved palms.

The open form has two decorative surfaces: the inside and the outside. The proportion between these two describes the form. It is this variety of proportions together with the pleasure we get from handling it that explains the popularity of this form. Tall, cylindrical forms offer large decorative surfaces both inside and out. The greater the height in relation to the diameter the less we see of the inside surface. Wide open forms, dishes or shallow bowls, offer an immediate view of the inside surface. The outside may also be decorated to be appreciated when the bowl is lifted up or placed on a reflective surface. Between these two extremes exist a wide variety of forms from the purely functional to the purely decorative.

Open forms are sometimes used as wall decorations. Commemorative or limited edition plates are examples of this. Usually the decoration is painted or transfers. Can you find examples of these? You might like to design a plate to be wall mounted. The surface should be high relief with very little of the plate surface undecorated. You could produce a broad cylindrical container. You might do this in clay using a slab, coiled or a thrown technique. You could then decorate it in relief, either the inside leaving the outside free of decoration, or the outside leaving the inside free. Can you comment on the way the decoration alters the function of the form?

Try to design a small bowl to fit into your cupped hands. Make it from clay in the simplest way you can. Does it require decoration or does the simplicity of the form please?

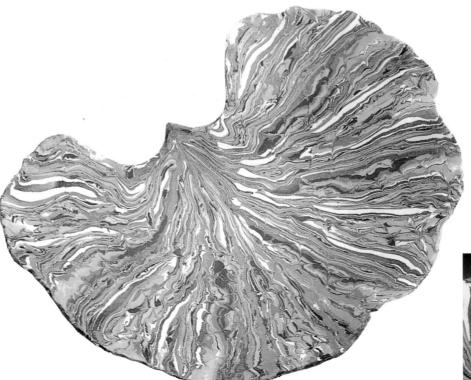

Virginia Mitcham, Halcyon Spring, 1991, *45.7 cm × 11.4 cm, ceramic/porcelain bowl.*

Virginia Mitcham, Halcyon Spring, *detail.*

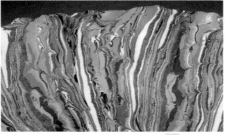

CLOSED FORMS

The closed form is a basic functional form. It is most commonly seen as a bottle, flask or perhaps a sealed jar. To give you an indication of the wide variety that this form can be found in, you might like to make a collection of glass bottles. These range from elaborate perfume bottles to the simple functional form of a wine bottle or a milk bottle. You might like to keep a record of your collection by drawing silhouettes. Within it you may find that some wine bottle forms are associated with different regions or countries. Look at the different bottle forms. Limit yourself to 75 cl wine bottles for this investigation. All have to contain a set quantity of liquid in a safe condition. The bottles therefore all have the same basic function. Collect as wide a range as you can. Look for the extremes of form. Can you find examples where the decoration of the form actually interferes with the function?

Lucie Rie, stoneware bottle, height 22.6 cm.

Craft potteries often sell storage jars or condiment sets. Perhaps you could compare the various forms that potteries in your area produce. Are they all similar?

Glass bottles are usually mass produced and are therefore mostly symmetrical. Standardised forms are cheaper and easier to produce. Ceramic bottles, even when thrown on the wheel, do not have to be symmetrical as they can be formed while still damp. The closed ceramic form has many possibilities, as shown by the examples on these two pages. In the case of these bottles, and most other closed forms, the main decorative area is the outside. They can, however, be cut into to reveal decorated interiors or opened up, like the wide fluted lip of the bottle by Lucie Rie. You could produce a series of small closed containers, perhaps to function as perfume bottles. Link your series by developing them in a single direction, i.e. getting rounder, getting taller, becoming less symmetrical or any other direction you can envisage. There should be at least three in your series. If formed from clay they could be pinched, thrown or coiled. The restricted opening that can be characteristic of this form could be sealed by a stopper or a cork. Do not try to decorate your surface. Try to please through the simple use of form.

Cecilia Parkinson, porcelain conical form, *18 cm high*, 1994.

Len Castle, hanging bottle.

DECORATIVE SURFACES

Siddig El'Nigoumi (b. 1931),
press moulded dish *20 × 18 cm.*

For decoration to be successful it must improve our appreciation of the form. Decoration which is not in sympathy with the form detracts from it and confuses the eye. Ceramics can be decorated through the use of colour, line, texture or pattern. These basic elements can be used together or, in certain circumstances, on their own. It does not need to be complex, in fact decoration is often most effective when understated.

The three pottery examples shown on these pages are decorative. Though the form is important it is secondary as they have all but ceased to be functional. It is the method of decoration used that minimises their function. The highly burnished dish shown above has a decoration scratched through the polished surface. This reveals the lighter colour of the clay beneath. The dramatic use of simple lines and earth colours reflects the influence of the artist's Sudanese background. The fine lines of the decoration make it impossible to visualise the dish in use as a container.

The hanging bottle, right, is decorated by heavy texture. This texture is brought alive by carefully placed lighting so that the deep shadows help bring the depth of the incisions into focus. The function of the bottle is restricted by the decoration cutting into the volume of the container.

The third example, below, is a bowl by Gary Wornell. This has been cut into as a part of its decoration. The cuts reduce the useful volume of the bowl and therefore its function, but they are an effective decorative device. The stencilled shapes in black are cut away from to leave a raised surface.

Len Castle, hanging bottle.

Decorative features do not have to detract from the function of the object. Experiment with different decorative effects on suitable 3D forms. You might like to use tile shapes or simple pinched or slab forms. Explore the idea of decoration towards extremes. You might use colour, line, texture or pattern. Look for examples from different cultures that show how much of these basic elements it is possible to use before the function becomes impaired. Often decoration is most effective when used with plain areas. This allows the eye to rest when examining the object.

Gary Wornell, raku bowl, 1985, *21 cm high.*

Fan-vaulted lantern of the Bell Harry Tower, Canterbury Cathedral.

SCULPTURE

Sculpture can be found in many places in the world around us, sometimes in very familiar surroundings. The photograph above shows a view of the ceiling of the central tower of Canterbury Cathedral. Completed at the end of the 15th century, Canterbury is typically Gothic in style with complex fan vaults which were carved in stone on the ground and later assembled to support the roof. Most churches have some form of sculpture within them, whether carved choir stalls, funeral monuments or complex roofing supports. Civic buildings have their plaques and even old town houses have moulded terracotta tiles built decoratively into them. Towns and villages often have sculptured war memorials, while nowadays large companies use sculpture as an expression of their prestige. You may also find local parks which 'house' the work of local sculptors.